Contents

New Article 1 1
Dedications 2
List of content 3
Preamble 5
About the author 6
The 5 gifts 8
Definition of the method 10
Section 1 Explore your mind 11
Set your goals 12
List of actions 14
The naked truth 15
Let's go dreaming 17
Invisible blocks 20
Section 2 Clear your mind 22
Wipe away your blocks 23
A New set of daily mindful habits 27
Avoid the continuous routine 29
Reality check 31
Section 3 Ready your mind 33
21 days to instill a habit 34
Strengthen your rocks 37
Actions speak louder 39
Understanding yourself better 41
You are the boss 44
Section 4 Mindful living 46
Awareness creates necessity for action 47
Becoming complete 49
Subconscious growth of self 51
Trust the universe 53
Section 5 Repeat 55
Finding your happy place 56
Authors' closing note 58
many thanks, to some of the participant of my method..........59
New Article 60

1.
2.
3.
4.
5.
6.
7.
8.
9.
10.
11.
12.
13.
14.
15.
16.
17.
18.
19.
20.
21.
22.
23.
24.
25.
26.
27.
28.
29.
30.
31.
32.
33.

A Guide to a Dream Life

by Olga Cooper

"Every second that we are breathing, we can change the route of our life. Feeling blessed is a choice not a given. Action and courage are a must in a successful plan."

List of content

List of content - 4
Preamble - 6
About the Author - 8
The 5 Gifts - 10
Definition of the method - 12

Section 1
Explore your mind
Set your goals - 14
The naked truth - 18
Let's go dreaming - 20
Invisible blocks - 24

Section 2
Clear your mind
Dealing with our blocks - 29
A new set of daily mindful habits - 35
Avoid the continuos routine - 39
Reality check - 41

Section 3
Ready your mind
21 days to instill a habit - 45
Strengthen your rocks - 48
Actions speak louder - 52
Understand yourself better - 55
You are the boss - 59

Section 4
Mindful living
Awareness creates necessity for action - 64
Conclusion - 67
Subconscious growth of self - 70
Trust the universe - 73

Section 5
Recap
Finding your happy place - 76
Authors' closing note - 79

Credits 80

Preamble

Do you feel as if your life has been going in circles?

Your dreams aren't becoming true as if everything is against you. ?

Your life isn't happy nor fulfilling no matter how hard you try ?

Your money is never sufficient, and doesn't stick around long enough for you to enjoy spending it?

Your personal relationships don't last long, or they last but aren't at the level you wish they were.

It seems that no matter what you do and how much time you spend thinking, planning and taking action?

You find yourself back to the same circumstances over and again?

There are many solutions out there to change and remedy your situation; you may have tried some of them already, yet you are nowhere close to achieving any of your dreams or goals.

You don't know how to get adequate answers.

Don't fret, this method is created by me, for those who want to realise their dreams into reality through belief, intention and action.

The process might seem unfamiliar to you at first, but once you learn what you are truly capable of, you would realize that for so long you have been intoxicating your own mind, and preventing yourself from reaching your potential and desires.
My guide takes you through a process of enabling your mind, to conceive and manifest things ideas and personal goals that were beyond your wildest imagination. Believe in the concept and it becomes clear to you.

This method will help you not only reach these goals, but also attain the life of your dreams.

About the author

Olga Cooper

A Russian born, with Irish adopted through work and life and now residing in Como, Italy.

Born in 1981, traveled the world through a job that my mother had. Have a younger sister.

High school in America, University in Ireland, Life worldwide.
Start of career in Ireland in real estate and financial sector with projects in London, Dublin, Nice and NYC .

Married to a king of Holograms whom I met 8 years ago when I messaged him to buy his company for my partner. Now we have 4 amazing kids, 3 of which are one year apart.

My book and method are unique purely because I am unique.
My favourite job is a door to door sales person which speaks a lot of my ability in communication skills.

During this transformational year of my life I had a pleasure to help more than 100 amazing humans worldwide and from all walks of life to level up and get the dream life they always desired by sharing my knowledge that now is a method.

Since i am 28 years old , I am a risk management consultant and work for myself. Helped many to multiply their wealth by x10 . I am able to see what others don't and that's my gift. In my book I assist you as a reader to see and outline the gifts that you have in order to get financial freedom and have your dreams come true by asking simple questions that reveal a lot of answers.

My book "A guide to a dream Life" helps to show you the ability our brain has and how we can use it to our advantage. When our head is able to listen to our desires, we are able to take action through understanding and connecting with our true self and with this I am able to motive you to take action.

Being positive and acting from a position of Love is my motto in life.

My life and I are unique and now I am ready to share it all.
I am on great terms with all of my exes and their families and my ex bosses are now my partners in several private projects and I believe it is my super power to not hold a grudge or be a victim.

I am blessed to know and have experienced lessons from top humans of this world and now I am ready to share the knowledge with hope that some would be inspired to take action towards their dream and trust that all is possible.

Only a year ago I was that person at the bottom and without hope left inside my mind and body, I started my journey with the support of my family and friends and here I am better than before and ready to Inspire and Shine. My story is from super top to ashes and back up, complete rebirth on all levels.
I love life and all that it has to offer.

Be fierce in loving yourself for you are amazing, and that will fuel your most desired dreams to come to life.

The confidence of being able to walk your path of life alone and without fears.

It takes two or more people to do things in a negative sense, yet it takes one person to change it all...

That's how I personally feel and what I believe in.
You   are   number   one

The 5 gifts

"Welcome to my guide to your Dream Life, and your future success, tried and tested by me, written for you."
Olga Cooper

One of my many goals of this book, is to show each and every one who would read it, that we all possess the following "5 Gifts" that help us on our journey to
a successful financial future.

The goal is to demonstrate to you how to find these gifts within you and have a disciplined action plan.

The "5 GIFTS" that we would explore and find are:

1. One that keeps you happy with your look, physical.

2. One that helps your inner child come out and create.

3. One that helps you understand and use information that is already inside of you and around you.

4. One that helps your brain to be happy and relaxed in order to operate more effectively.

5.   One to help you see money opportunities - a gift that you are able to see inside of you and use it to benefit yourself: financially. Explanation- a gift/ability that you can sell, exchange or give as gift. All of the above isenergy, and the exchange of it will benefit your life, and get you closer to a dream life.

My belief is :

«When you know and feel that you are destined for greatness, your potential haunts you, and if you don't see it or even worse ignore it, your life becomes difficult.

The ideas and dreams keep you up and make all that you do a challenge. You need to manifest your higher purpose and become one with all 5 Gifts and that's done by raising your vibrations through daily actions».

To me, courage and the ability to act are the most attractive qualities anyone can possess.

In my daily life , I am all about improving finances and seeking opportunities, I see them, smell them, and know them like it is blood going through my veins. On top of it, I excel at crisis management, and determine the potential of people I meet , and prepare action plans based on their situation. The higher the level of success reached the more fun I have. The more basic the level is, the more potential for growth I can establish and help them capitalize on.

I love life and all that it has to offer. I can help you!

Definition of the method

Definition of the method

IF You are a person looking to help yourself out of a rut, or you are looking to upgrade your already comfortable lifestyle, This book is for you, guaranteed. It helps you adjust your life so you see the opportunities all around you, your pains and worries will start to fade and be replaced by joy and comfort.

This method has enhancing effects on all levels. It will not make you perfect in the absolute meaning of the term. There is no such a thing as a perfect human being, because if there were, then the chances for improvement would be non-existent, and you wouldn't be reading this book.

At this moment, you should take a moment of reflection, and acknowledge this fact:
No one is perfect and no one will ever be, all we are is a work in progress.

Don't be discouraged by the fact that you're not perfect, no one is. Instead, realize that it is very dangerous to think that you are perfect, at any moment in life. This kind of thinking pulls you toward a comfort zone in your mind, this leads to complacency, followed by mediocre achievements, and eventually dissatisfaction. This is a negative emotion that triggers self-sabotage patterns, and we all want to avoid this happening.

"My Method" enables you to manifest an ideal dream life. This way you are prepared for your bright upcoming future. At the same time, it provides you with the necessary tools to keep an eye on your progress, and adjust your personal plan as you go along.

It works directly with your conscious and subconscious in order to show you how to connect your head, heart and soul, so you are in control of your thoughts and emotions. It also explores the spiritual side to strengthen beliefs, and whilst doing all of that, it encourages you to improve and maintain your physique. Our goal is to have a perfectly balanced compass- an alignment between head, heart and soul.
It is very important that you go through the book step by step, in the order it is written. Skipping chapters and taking a peak into future pages is counterproductive and must be avoided. Stay in the moment, enjoy!

"The Guide to Your Dream Life" shows you that when you do everything from a position of love, you are unstoppable. I believe that **when your thoughts and feelings about yourself, match the thoughts and feelings of other people about you, especially people, in your close circle, then you are successful and self-confident.**

Section 1

Explore your mind

Explore your mind

Set your goals

Like every person on this earth, you have experienced disappointment and many of your dreams or ideas did not see the light. The fact that you are not alone in this journey, doesn't mean stop trying. You might have noticed that the older we get and the more failure we go through, settling down or settling for less creeps in and becomes a controlling force .Consequently we follow the crowd and become less ambitious and stop pursuing new dreams, simply because we get exhausted, from trying. We instead start fearing for and protecting the little things that we already have by playing safe. This becomes the most dangerous enemy of our own progress.

Here and now, it is the time you start trusting yourself and the universe. I want to show you how to recognize the existing connection between both (HERE AND NOW), and harness its unlimited powers.

Please see a line below and write your current financial net worth and the date (one figure in any currency you like, based on the amount you currently have to live on). Remember to be very honest while writing this figure, it is your book and no one else would see this except you. Once you start reaping the fruits of your success, it might be nice to look back and identify how unbelievably fast this method helped you to see and improve your finances and life goals.

Current Net Worth _____ date _____

It is time to close your eyes for a while – it could be few seconds to few minutes – and imagine a figure that you think would be achievable from your point of view, that would make you feel financially safe and live well as per the standards you wish for. Don't write this figure yet because it's too early, but let us call it your goal for now. Remember this figure clearly.

Now close your eyes again, and imagine that the whole universe has engaged all its' resources and infinite powers and possibilities in order to help you achieve your goal; With this new limitless potential, would you still stick to the figure you had in mind? Personally I would aim for a higher figure to ultimately achieve more goals, and have more challenges to overcome, but that's just me. You might like to set a more conservative figure at first, until you are comfortable with your progress. Everyone is different. Remember this important point , there is no right or wrong.

A moment of truth for you now, a decision needs to be taken and the time has come for you to write your dream figure – the initial one you had in mind or the new one you opted for – anywhere you like on the page.

A dream figure of Net

worth_____date_____

It was easy, wasn't it?

Congratulations, you now have a start point and a goal set financially. To go from start to end goal, you always need to draw a roadmap and devise a plan of action.

For this purpose you now need to go the next empty page titled List of Actions.

Go ahead and write a list of actions that you should repeat daily for a minimum of 21 consecutive days. These actions help you reach your goal. Such actions should be about you, your growth, your well-being, new things you would like to try, and everything else you wish to be doing for you, and only you. (For example : I would exercise for 30 minutes a day; I would read a book a week; I would write down all of my expenses and spend less; I would prepare a plan for the next day in the evening; etc)

Explore your mind

List of actions

Write your list of actions for the upcoming 21 days minimum, more is always better.

<u>21 days to instill a new habit</u>
<u>12 weeks to get used to it</u>
<u>6 months for it to become a part of the routine</u>
<u>1 year to desire it</u>
<u>2 + years for it to become part of YOU</u>

Explore your mind

The naked truth

> *"Are you moving towards what matters to you?*
> *Or moving towards what matters to others?"*

By doing the previous actions and tasks, you have identified now that you are **number one** as you should have always been. You had to ignore this fact for far too long, putting others ahead of you. Time to change your priorities and perspectives, time to appreciate the following realities:

> You are the center of your own universe and without you in it, your universe would cease to exist, so there is no point in putting someone else ahead of you. Your life's meaning lies within your existence, so honor it by caring for yourself first and by striving to achieve it.
>
> Our time on earth is limited. Make your time worthwhile by reaching your full potential, and start **now** by focusing on the goals you outlined on the previous pages. Through my work that lead me to creating this guide, I have heard this from everyone I guided and simultaneously learned from: It is an utterly unforgivable mistake to dedicate our lives to others, **no greatness is achieved by ignoring ourselves and our own needs and aspirations.** History and society teach us to be compassionate, feel for the others, help and support those in need and that's not wrong. We should definitely do our best, and yes there is loads of happiness in giving, but it shouldn't come at the cost of us putting ourselves anywhere except first place. Wouldn't you be happier if you preserved yourself, cared for your growth, received more, and consequently became able to give more, in abundance and without fear?

> You are the only one responsible for achieving your goal. No one would come to your help or rescue unless there is something in it for them, i.e. an emotional or physical advantage, or financial gain. If this sounds strange to you now, it means you are not ready yet. Don't worry about that, people often go into denial and disbelief at first, this is because your ego still has control over your thoughts, and it is resistant to change especially at this stage. The truth will come to you when time is appropriate.
> Your attitude will determine what happens with your goals and achievements; to you these goals are everything you have longed for, so I recommend you get ready, for fiercely leading a life of pursuit and dedication, free of excuses. Have you ever heard a winner giving excuses? No – only losers and underachievers do so, and the *"new you"* sets sail now on a winners journey.

You must be wondering, what about my family? My friends? My partner? My network of contacts, my social entourage. The answers are easy:

> If you fail and keep failing, it puts you in a vulnerable position of being in need, which makes you unhappy, and as a result you feel anger and dissatisfaction, and you lash out on people around you. In reality, what you feel and see are the things that bother you the

most inside, and now with the knowledge, you are strong enough to outline the minuses (-) and turn them into pluses (+)

It is of the highest importance at this stage that you consciously accept a fact that you might have heard earlier, in one way or another: *"You were born alone and you die alone"*. What happens between these two major events of your life is entirely up to you. You are your own number one.

Explore your mind

Let's go dreaming

Imagine you are an aspiring young actor or actress, whose career has been somewhat "OK" performance so far; by purchasing my book, you contracted an agent that already got you the deal you have been waiting for; you have been spotted by a producer called The Universe and you are now given the chance to write, direct and take on the lead role in the new series called: "The rest of your life". What you decide to write in the script right now, how you decide to direct it, who are the other cast members and the way you would perform your role is all up to your imagination and action.

As a member of your audience, I look forward to witnessing an award-winning performance, and I would expect nothing short of a thriller filled with action, life, events, unexpected turns and the courage to be bold so when you go writing the script, please remember this: *"Do not limit your challenges, challenge your limits"*.

Just a while ago, you performed the exercise of setting a financial goal and figure that you should be reminding yourself of, very often and with clear intentions of achieving it. Wouldn't it be nice to have the lifestyle that matches or even supersedes that goal?

Before you go forward, take a moment to make yourself aware that my guide is not about how fast you read the book, but about how effectively you would use the tools given to you, therefore don't rush this part especially, savor it instead, and start constructing your future on the solid foundation of believing in your capabilities and the universe.

"As you have decided, so it shall be". Right now, you have the means to do anything you want, so go forward building the empire of your dreams.

On the coming empty page, I want you to write down the ingredients of your already successful life. Write everything in the present tense.

A guide to help you write it all down:

✳ I am, I have, I want, I do, I use, I eat, I own and all the verbs that you chose to write should be in the present tense.

✳ Start by thinking about the countries you would like to frequently visit, the city or cities you would like to live in, the kind of properties you would like to own – is it a luxurious mansion, an expensive villa, house and so on..

✳ Think about the facilities and options available for you in your place of living, it could be a tennis court, a helipad with your own helicopter, an Olympic swimming pool, a spa, your private beach, or own ski slopes, anything you desire to have, the sky is the limit, and imagine all that comes with the staff necessary to maintain and operate for your comfort..

✳ Now think about the businesses you own and run, the offices and all kind of facilities related to your businesses, imagine your main personal office, the space, the scenery from the large windows, the furniture in it, your desk and what items are on the desk, the colors, the stationary, the smell of all of it combined. ..

✳ Write down also the hobbies and kind of entertainment you would like to pursue for your leisure, the fleet of cars and the best drivers at your disposal.

✳ Describe how you are dressed, head to toe in details. Write down how you see your partner/spouse within all this. ..

✳ Write further and further until the page is full or you can't dream anymore.

One very important task you must fulfill while writing all that down. For every item you write, close your eyes for as long as you want, and try to visualize the most vivid image your mind can construct of it. It could be an item that you have seen and for long time desired to have, or an item that your mind just designed for you.

As much as it's important to engrave this image in your mind, it is crucial to remember the way it felt when you were visualizing this image. There are generally 2 categories of feelings that you would experience:

Steady feelings like happiness, joy, excitement, cheerfulness, delight and we'll mark this category with the letter "S" for steady.

Unstable feelings like ambiguity, doubt, hesitation, fear, undecidedness and we'll mark this category with the letter "U" for unstable.

Here's an example:

I close my eyes and imagine the following sentence that I just wrote and have big smile in my heart, seeing the image too very clear and bright (I mark it with "S")

<u>*I own a Rolls Royce "S"*</u>
I close my eyes and imagine the following sentence that I just wrote and have tingly feeling, seeing the image blurred (I mark it with "U")

<u>*I am flying to the moon on my own spaceship "U"*</u>

Now that you have outlined the future that you desire and noted down your "S's"& "U's", I would like to briefly explain the significance of these markings. The things that you see brightly and happily and steadily are the things most likely to happen to you the fastest, while the other feelings indicate your uncontrolled disbelief in the items written next to them, and that is due to an unidentified subconscious trigger that is governed by your psychological patterns and programs, they will take a little longer to achieve.
Each of the feelings you had is accompanied with a certain chemical produced by the brain, which triggers or gets triggered by a thought or reaction to a thought, stored in the memory

of the body. Right now, we will not expand further on that as it's the turf of Neuroscientists.

Don't be alarmed though with this discovery about yourself and your items marked "U", on the contrary take it as an opportunity to address these feelings, and the subconscious programs and patterns related to them. You will be guided through such procedures in future chapters.

New Task: It is highly recommended for now that you use a voice recorder with calm music in the background, to read calmly, slowly and with your warmest voice all the items marked with "S" making them sound like a guided meditation made by you for you, your self-made mantra. When you are done recording, save the file and go add a task to listen to it on the list of daily actions you have created

<u>My "S"s & My "U"s</u>

_____   _____

_____   _____

_____   _____

_____   _____

_____   _____

_____   _____

Explore your mind

Invisible blocks

Welcome to the last chapter of this section. It is supposed to be the final stage of decisively exploring your mind, it is related to the items marked with *"U"*s on your list, the feelings you have identified and the consequences of these findings.

Now read very carefully and remember the guidelines, as you have to do this exercise for every item on your list of *"U"*s, and any other new item you might identify and stumble upon along the way; as you go meditating and thinking through after meditation, you would figure out more feelings and events that you were unaware of but still would have to deal with.

At first, it might feel like the labyrinth of your past, events that your conscious mind might have forgotten about, and the darkest moments in your life where you have suffered deeply, to the point that you still hold residual feelings or traumas. Such feelings could be fear, anger, hatred, envy, grief, self-pity etc. and from now on we refer to them as your *"blocks"*.

It will feel like a bumpy ride and you will need lots energy to go through it, the courage to face your demons and deepest fears, and the power to deal with whatever will be found. Although it might be unpleasant to deal with past traumas and repressed memories, it is a necessary evil that can't be left unaddressed; these blocks are the hidden enemies of you, hence wise to turn them into allies and sources of power.

This should not be worrying nor alarming, and even this part can be done smoothly. I believe that you have all what it takes to conquer your past. Be reminded always that you are your number one, the captain of your own destiny and that the journey you have started requires all your wit and wisdom to successfully reach your goals and full potential.

Once you manage through meditation to reach such events and feelings, note them down on a new list called "my blocks", very clearly and just bullet points:
> *What was the event that you saw or remembered from your past?*
> *What was the feeling or mix of feelings related to that specific event?*

As an example, you could remember the event of failure at work for which you received disciplinary action. The feeling you could have had is possibly anger with the way your boss handled the situation. When you come back from your meditation, write down with clear language: I failed at work and was angry with my boss. It is known that "a well-defined problem is half solved" especially when done in writing.

Multiple sessions of meditation might be required for you to identify all your blocks and write them down. No person in history was able to address all their issues through taking short cuts, but if you do the work properly, you will earn the rewards. This is critical for your progress and for reaching your end goal.

In future steps, my guide will bring you back to these moments you have just identified in your subconscious mind, enabling you to address them, the feelings that are connected to them and the hidden patterns/programs originating from them.

For the time being, keep the search going and the deeper you reach and more you find the happier and prouder of yourself you would be; with every finding, you go one step closer to reaching the destination you have set for yourself.

Irrespective of the how long or extensive this specific list has become, and at the start of every session, I want you to read the list entirely as if it's someone else's' list, and try to detach any feeling that might triggered by any item on the list whenever possible. Put an asterisk next to any items you couldn't detach yourself from feelings when you read them.

Be prepared to move to the next section of the book by the time you think you have identified all your hidden blocks. At this stage, there are three important takeaways that I need you to note:

> *The list is not final yet. You might think it is, but more items would most probably be triggered in the very near future, and for sure would require further processing.*

> *The items that you have marked with an asterisk (*) are the toughest ones you would have to deal with, so for them prepare you're **"A game"** as within them lie big possibilities.*

> *The items you didn't associate any feelings with, and didn't mark with an asterisk are most probably trivial, and are part of the ego that didn't want to let go of them. Your ego in this case is acting like an autoimmune disease that is causing you more damage than protection. As you have no emotional attachments to them I suggest you control your ego in order to get rid of them and ensure they don't come back.*

At the end of the first section in this book, you must be feeling proud of your achievements so far. In a matter of few days, you have managed to at least:

> *Set new goals for your life, knowing that you can achieve them by believing and putting the work towards them. Identify yourself as your **"Number One"** in your life.*

> *Compile a list of activities (mental, physical and probably spiritual) that you are practicing daily, and maybe more than once a day in order to help bringing you close to your dreams.*

> *Identify your dreams that you believe in, and start directing your energy and organizing yourself and your life towards achieving them.*

> *Identify unpleasant fragments of your past that need to be addressed or processed, in order to mitigate their toxic effect on your present and future.*

> *There is nothing to be ashamed of, we all have our pluses and minuses; you should be proud you are dealing with your minuses bravely.*

> *Recognize that your ego is not helping you, it is just holding on to unimportant negative things you shouldn't even care about, but it is instead working against you, and for you to achieve your future goals, you would need to befriend your ego, in order to focus on your goals instead and the actions leading you towards them.*

Section 2

Clear your mind

Clear your mind

Dealing with our blocks

Many of you are doubting yourself right now or the journey you are on. Fortunately for you, I've already done the process, and I can assure you that with discipline, going through the plan of action, and with the magic of the meditation process, the results you are expecting will arrive sooner than you think, as long as you trust yourself, trust the universe and keep putting yourself as your own first priority, as your number one.

With newly found strength and refreshed energy that you recently acquired – or maybe enhanced if you had previous experience – through ability to meditate and dream about your future with clarity, and focus on yourself and your goals with clear intent, you are moving up the levels of your own intellect. By tapping into these resources, you are now fully prepared and equipped to dive right into the process of dealing with your blocks list and removing any psychological feelings or triggers that you have already identified and listed.

If at this stage you do feel that the process of removing your blocks on your own is incomprehensible, you should work on shaking away this feeling. You are capable of surfing your own subconscious mind without the need of any guidance, as well as, strong enough to face anything you might encounter – you are the boss.

The purpose of the meditation and dreaming is for you to reach a memory identified on your blocks list, imagine the moment as it was, allow it a few seconds and then substitute it with a positive and pleasant outcome. This is how you turn your subconscious enemies from the past into your allies for the future.

I will give you two major illustrative examples of what could be written on the list, and how you are able to convert the negative into positive during your meditation and dreamy process.

First example, is when the negative is related to a person: you could have identified and listed that you are holding feelings of grudge or hatred toward someone who hurt you in your past (i.e. a bully from school, a relative with a very bad attitude, a teacher with some kind of complex, etc.). What you need to do is, once you reach a place where you feel safe in your subconscious mind (no matter what the place is and how it looks like, this is where you are the boss, you completely trust yourself and the universe and you have nothing to fear), you would need to invite that person, to come and meet with you and to do the following:

> _Prepare a gift that you would like to give to that person. For every person you would meet you could give a different gift. You are very rich and very generous and very creative and anything you wish for is at your reach._

Visualize taking all the negative feelings you have towards that specific person, and then put them inside that item.

Visualize wrapping this as a very beautiful gift.

Visualize the person clearly in front of you; how are they dressed? how are they looking at you? Are they seated/standing? Are they happy/sad? Etc.

Shake their hand and say to that person: thank you for coming to meet me, I am glad to see you; I have invited you here today because I have a gift to give to you, but before that, I would like to thank you for the lessons you gave me, for the way you made me feel (state all the negative feelings they caused you in front of them), and thank you for listening to me right now.

I am now stronger than before, I am now much happier than before and I don't need those feelings you made me feel all this long, so I give them back to you with gratitude. I forgive you for anything you have done to me and ask for your forgiveness in return.

Visualize giving the gift to that person saying: here I prepared this expensive and beautiful gift for you. Please take it, enjoy it and now is the time for you to leave as I need to be somewhere else.

Bid them farewell and watch them leave.

Remember that your intentions are clear and your energies are clean, hence do not try to give back the feelings out of spite or revenge, this is counterproductive and would replace the negative with negative. Always return the feelings with love and forgiveness, for in forgiveness lies your power and freedom.

Second example, is when the negative is related to a situation: Traumatic events are usually marked by a sense of horror, helplessness, serious injury, or the threat of serious injury or death. Natural disasters, such as a tornado, hurricane, fire, or flood. Witness of death, sexual assault, physical assault.
Such events happened to the majority of us, and many of us wouldn't experience emotional damage directly exhibited in one's behavior but still unknowingly carry the weight of a traumatic event very far in our subconscious.

The process here would be slightly different, as you don't have a person to deal with, so you would be communicating directly with the universe:

Prepare a gift item that you would like to give to the universe.

Visualize taking all the negative feelings you have towards that specific situation, and then put them inside that gift item.

Visualize wrapping this as a very beautiful gift.

Visualize yourself standing in the vast emptiness of the universe where nothing is there but everything is there at the same time (your imagination shall guide you to what the universe looks like to you).

Hold the gift on both palms at your chest level and repeat the following: thank you for blessing me and allowing me to be here, I am glad and grateful; I have come here today because I have a gift to give to you, but before that, I would like to thank you for the lessons you gave me, for the way these lessons made me feel (state all the negative feelings caused to you by the specific traumatic event), and thank you for listening to me right now. I am now stronger than before, I am now much happier than before and I don't need those feelings that I carried all this long, so I give them back to you with gratitude.

Visualize releasing the gift item to the universe: here I prepared this expensive and beautiful gift for you. Please take it, I don't need it, but I desire and I expect to receive a positive gift in return (you can even state the gift you are expecting to receive).

Once you feel that the gift and the negative feelings left your sight, thank the universe and return to your conscious self.

After you have done one successful reversal of emotions, it should become easier for you to do it and more importantly, you will start feeling immediately liberated and lighter; you will recognize that all the negative emotions you have been carrying this far, have been poisoning you from inside and you will start craving to get rid of all the items on the list, as soon as possible.

Be prepared for the possibility of encountering and identifying new items, that you might need to add to the blocks list, and deal with on a separate session.

For this new set of sessions to be done, here are the specific instructions on how to manage such intensive and emotional meditating and dreaming sessions:

Start by preparing your meditation environment as illustrated in the meditation chapter and as you have so far practiced.

Make sure your legs are not crossed (preferably touching the ground).

Your palms should be facing upwards so you can allow yourself to receive, as well as allow yourself to let go.

Think of an anchor that you would always focus on in case you get distracted. This could be anything you would like to visualize for a moment before you start your session (this could be your lotus flower that you visualized in previous meditation).

Clearly state your intention for the meditation session (we have gone through illustrative examples earlier). This should be clearly articulated before you go into your subconscious. The universe is listening and is ready to help, but requires clear communication and clean intentions.

Start by regulating your deep breathing. Close your eyes focus on your third eye, then go inside yourself from there.

Once you reach a safe place, you then go ahead and focus on either the person or the situation that you intend to deal with in this session and proceed to reversing the negative energy into positive energy.

Keep focusing on your regular and deep breath, and your anchor if need be.

Once you feel that you have successfully fulfilled your intention of the session, take few more deep breaths and come back to consciousness.

Never underestimate the intensity of any of these sessions, and never let the power of habit sneak in to your mind. No matter how many successful sessions of emotional reversal you have gone through, always remember the safety tips at the end of a meditation:

Drink lots of water.

Lie down in a relaxed position (preferably on your back) and let the new emotions sink in.

Do not move immediately after the session.

Allow your motoric functions and physical balance to return to you first, enjoy the moment.

Avoid sudden movements (sudden turning, sitting down or standing up) after you start moving again.

As this set of sessions might stretch over days or maybe weeks, given the fact that no one can face all their blocks at once, and also depending on the number of items you have listed. It is recommended that you start reading and practicing during the next chapter

This is the most tiring part of the process and once you feel very confident that you have gone through it, everything after shall be done smoothly and very easily.

Clear your mind

A New set of daily mindful habits

There are many ways for you to clear your mind, increase your energy levels and positive emotions. As we have established beforehand, you are undergoing the process for your own   development, for the fulfillment of your dreams and desires and because of that, every step you do must be accompanied with belief – ***in yourself and the universe*** –, ***trust*** - ***in yourself and the universe*** – and clear and clean intentions. This chapter is no different as you are required to maintain top levels of energy every time you move forward.

You were always told that in order to achieve, you need to do hard work and complete tasks with so much effort, with high focus, patience and resilience; these are awesome qualities; however, you were made to believe that without hardship there will be no fruits to reap, and this had you programmed to expect no results unless the path was tough. Although there is high esteem for all the hard work and hard workers, it does not mean that there could be no exceptions.

So, my recommendation to you is, try to think of everything you are doing as a pleasant task, as part of your joyful mission (even the straining and draining sessions); as you are aiming to become whole, you need to allow yourself to embrace the positive and the negative – one cannot exist without the other –, they are both inevitable and you are redefining your character by the way you handle both of them. If you want a happy life, you need to put joy into everything you do.

Alongside your ongoing campaign against your blocks, you would be better off by starting to add new habits to your daily actions. The sessions are intense and they are draining lots of your energy almost on a daily basis, and for you to be able to joyfully continue further, you definitely need to reload and recharge.

Here are some of the options, endorsed by the majority of people I worked with or learned from:

> *Improve your sleep quality This is not necessarily long sleep, but resting sleep. The majority of high performers, overachievers, rich and famous people, their sleep is not long in time but deep in quality. Everyone can observe their sleep patterns, and once you accept that not everybody needs a minimum of 8 hours daily, then you understand how many hours you need to sleep daily, in order to feel rested and energetic. You might feel unbalanced for the first 2 or 3 days if you start changing your sleep patterns, however, once you find your own rhythm, you would immediately notice the enormous increase in both your energy and your mental effectiveness.*

> *Meditation and dreamy sessions that are focused on self-affirmation Since I was a child I realized the power and the impact of positive thinking on ones' self. I can't emphasize enough the importance of self-affirmation and admiration, if you don't have it then you don't have true love for anyone or anything else, and any form of love you think you are experiencing is just an illusion. It is said that "when you take care of yourself, you start feeling better, looking better and attracting better".*

> *Consciously complement your self-affirmation that you practice in meditative state; you would need to emboss it in your conscious mind along with confidence and positive emotions. You also need to start training your mind to attract money, and send energy towards money opportunities, hence you may want to start tuning your mindset to the following:*
>   *I attract money and see money opportunities around me.*

>   *I always have enough. If not in my possession, I believe it's coming to me.*

>   *I am not afraid to spend, for the flow of money towards me is endless.*

"Passion is the source of energy that fuels our minds and souls. Once you find a it, you start steering thoughts, energy actions and focus towards achieving it".

When you build on your rocks and capitalize on your positive habits, you start becoming more mindful of your emotional and your physical sensors, more aware of what is happening within your body and mind, and your surroundings.

You then would be able to advance your mindfulness. Every time you consciously notice an emotion or feeling, you need to close your eyes and ask specific questions and direct them to that particular feeling or emotion that you are experiencing.

The following 3 questions are the most important of our lives and this method. If you become automatic in asking yourself these questions or any other that you like, before you react to a situation, your abundance flow would never stop. As learning to detach emotions in life situations, brings opportunities and success in all areas of our life. Questions are always a good idea as they work as a protection screen to our soul and heart and are kind to our mind. No need to guess, just ask!

Why are you here?

What are you trying to tell me?

What are you trying to teach me?

Then you need to wait few seconds after every question; you most probably will start seeing shapes and/or images, or even hear voices. If you don't see or hear anything, you may repeat the question couple of times (there are times where really nothing will happen). The interesting part of this mindfulness exercise is when you do hear or see something, it is usually answers that you are receiving in response to questions or wishes you have put out earlier to the universe, and your skill in mapping these answers to the respective question or wish will shape up with time.

It has been proven that practicing mindfulness, self-affirmation and positive thinking with conviction can truly empower a person to achieve. If you have doubt about the efficiency of mindfulness, I invite you to compare it to the impact of stress and negative thinking; they both are instigated by thoughts.

A simple negative though even when you are sitting alone could trigger the brain to produce stress chemicals even though there is no real danger around you. Stress – when repetitive and not controlled – would start leading to misbalance of the body and its vital functions, causing damage to the nervous system and eventually result in some form of illness (medical research estimates as much as up to 90 percent of illness is related to or caused by stress).

If a negative thought could be at the root of illness, a positive though could be at the root of healing, of reversing – almost untreatable – medical conditions. Yes, this also has been scientifically proven via research. Another thought worth mentioning here, if positive thinking was proven to heal the body and the mind, why not use it to prevent the body and the mind from falling ill? Why not use it for the advancement of our body and mind? Since we all experience both negative and positive thoughts, it is only up to us to choose which ones to fuel. I know the choice is obvious and I promise you that the fruits and benefits of being well and achieving are worth fighting for.

As you go on becoming more mindful, asking questions and receiving answers more often, your brain and body become more and more attuned to the hormones of happiness, producing them every time you think positively or every time you suppress a negative thought or emotion. At a certain time, mindfulness becomes an inseparable part of your lifestyle both in conscious and subconscious/meditative state. Once it becomes effortless, you would start feeling like **you are plugged into the source, exchanging information gracefully and blissfully, like your brain is equipped with high speed chip that sends and receives data momentarily.**

You must have heard of people who operate on higher frequencies, or maybe with an open third eye, they see things that others can't and know things that others don't. This all stems from being mindful, in control of your emotions and in sync with your mind. It doesn't take necessarily long time or extensive practice for a person to become wired and connected, some people find this state of being very quickly.

Clear your mind

Avoid the continuous routine

When you become mindful and connected, you increase the range or your vision and it becomes multidimensional, you are no longer using just your eyes to see and perceive your surroundings and horizons. You no longer have blind spots, you are aware of all the information crossing your sphere and nothing skips you.

In this chapter , we are going to establish that long term routine, will prompt the return of blind spots and will put you in harm's way. Definitely we are not talking about the routine of a medication course for chronic disease, but the kind of routine that becomes redundant after a while (i.e. if you have been running for a while, change it to swimming or cycling).

First let us clarify the distinction between habit and routine. As humans, we are deeply convinced that we are creatures of habit, and that recurrence and habitual repetition are required for us to learn and train our mind or body. This is absolutely true and we will get into the importance of the habit in a future chapter.

Habit is defined in the dictionary as *"a settled or regular tendency or practice, especially one that is* **hard to give up***"*. The psychological definition is *"context-behavior associations in memory that develop as people repeatedly experience rewards for a given action in a given context.* **Habitual behavior does not require supporting goals and conscious intentions**".

Habits are essential to us. They can increase our odds of achieving our goals and maintaining a certain lifestyle. Habits shape our life far more than we probably realize.

"We are what we repeatedly do. Excellence, then, is not an act, but a habit". Aristotle

Routine on the other hand, is not essential on the long run and on the contrary, could prove dangerous and threatening to the mindful living. It is defined as *"a usual order and way of doing something, performed as part of a regular procedure"* *(actions or tasks executed as per certain timetable).*

Routine helps us reduce the stress of coping with change, and is needed to create and instill healthy habits over a specified period of time, and by making an anticipated decision about a course of action, the brain then would avail of mental resources that are freed by routine for other tasks. Once the habit is on, the routine must disappear.

When followed for longer than required, routine leads to a sense of steadiness and comfort, it can consequently make us complacent as we stop paying attention to the actions or tasks we are doing. This obliviousness would decrease our ability to notice things, and hence the outcome would be the blind spots we previously mentioned, the laziness in the brain and then the disruption of mindfulness.

As much as it's important for stress management, short time goals and for introducing new habits to your new lifestyle, routine shall never become continuous or permanent. Be aware of negative words, they become your thoughts, then your thoughts turn into negative habits and you go back to square one.

Clear your mind

Reality check

Gain insight into your personality and the impact of my guide so far. Your answers to the below questions need to be based on complete honesty. It is important that you consider your desires, and observe of your reactions to various events as a basis of validation for answering questions generally. For this exercise specifically, I ask you to fire out the answer immediately after having read the question, without thinking, second guessing and involving your mind – the answers must be from the heart – and as you would see, it's a simple YES or NO set of questions.

This is not a psychological evaluation quiz, though it might feel like one. Your time is very scarce and very important; hence we should treat it as such and therefore, the questions are designed and simply aimed for you to check your progress and adjust if need be.

Remember this: It's your book, your mind, your dreams and your life, so be vigorously honest with yourself and with answering the below questions.

Question   Yes/No

Do you feel more positive about yourself/your life? ❑ ❑

Do you think differently about other people? ❑ ❑

Do you notice any difference in the way you treat people? ❑ ❑

Did you like all your activities? ❑ ❑

Do you feel any changes in your creative side? ❑ ❑

Do you feel you can handle stress and anxiety differently by now? ❑ ❑
Do you feel better within your body or about your physique? ❑ ❑

Do you feel like you have more energy for your day every day?

Your answers should give you an indication whether to adjust any of your ongoing activities or not; so, if you answered yes to all the questions, keep charging forward as you are and conquer your new self. If you answered no to any of the questions, then note the following:

<u>*If you answered no to the first question, you are still not believing in your own abilities, and hence you are endangering the possibility of your own progress. Shift more time and focus on believing in yourself.*</u>

If you answered no to the second question, you still don't have enough confidence to allow yourself to have your own opinion about others. We have already established that your comfort and development are far more important than anything or anyone else.

If you answered no to the third question, you are still intimidated by the others and not daring to treat them on the basis of you being number one.

You need to find out who were your first intimidators and deal with them on a meditation session.

If you answered no to the fourth question, you are still resisting the change but this is not a scary point, change is most of the time uncomfortable.
If you answered no to the fifth question, you are still not thinking with your heart and not allowing spontaneity. Start spending more time on hobbies and things that you always wanted to do but never found the time for.
If you answered no to the sixth question, you are still not dealing properly with your emotions and you are not being mindful about your breathing.

Take few deep breaths whenever you feel stressed or anxious and keep breathing deeply until you feel better; you can do the deep breathing with closed eyes, asking the 3 questions and trying to find answers as you learned earlier.

If you answered no to the seventh question, you need to work on better accepting and loving yourself, as you are and then putting a serious plan and schedule to change to your desired shape/weight etc. if you have been trying unsuccessfully, it is time you invest in hiring professional help, like a personal trainer, getting on yoga courses, customized diet changes, etc.

If you answered no to the eighth question, then most probably you are still not sleeping, sporting or meditating enough. It is mandatory that you sleep your own needed number of hours, no more no less, it's crucially important to exercise in order to elevate your energy levels, and as you might have noticed, when you meditate to convey a positive wish and a happy quest, you end up receiving an awful lot of energy after each session.

You should at this point – after answering the questions – be proud of yourself. Obviously and simply because you are either on the high-speed lane if you answered all questions with yes, or because you have been so honest and open to determine where you are lacking, and going ahead with plans and actions to adapt and continue forward.

If you have answered no to 3 or more questions, an alarm should be raised within you. You would need to adjust your track and for that, you need to screen back all what you have been doing – kind of auditing all your activities so far – and determine whether you need to:

Work harder to compensate the areas with insufficient results.

Perhaps seek professional assistance in identifying and addressing your deepest fears and blocks.

Section 3

Ready your mind

Ready your mind

21 days to instill a habit

"Habitual behavior does not require supporting goals and conscious intentions". It is a form of automatic behavior that people repeat, because it is easy, comfortable or rewarding. You must have heard the expression *"Humans are creatures of habit".* As we grow up and develop to our adult personalities, we're simultaneously developing behaviors and habits that will stay with us for a lifetime.

You must have noticed that the new exercises you started doing recently are becoming easier with repetition. By you going forward, you would find that some of these exercises have already turned into automatic behaviors and effortless actions.

Go on and add new activities. It could be new physical, mental or spiritual exercise, new hobbies, etc. I recommend reading more, it's always meaningful and beneficial. Take an evening walk – on your own sometimes and the longer the better – it helps you clear your mind and refill your mental energy, especially if you take a moment to gaze at the sky, and draw your dream life up there. Have a delicious meal (try for one that is healthy for you since we are talking about regular activities). Exercise daily *(20 minutes a day – better than nothing – if you cannot afford longer time).* Expose yourself to the sun as often as possible. Spend quality time (not just time) with your better half. Give compliments to people.

The activities that you could add and turn into habits are countless. These new habits that you are adding to your being are without a doubt essential, for your current and ongoing progress, and for your future mental energy, as they directly interfere with your hormones of happiness:

Once you enable your habits to become automatic, you have successfully turned your mindset upwards and positioned yourself for a life of happiness, wealth and health *(what everybody wished you on almost every occasional/celebratory e-mail or message and you kept wondering why you are not achieving them).*

It might seem very hard at the beginning as every single one of these hormones/chemicals is produced by the brain as a reaction to different events/triggers, and combining all of these events/triggers in a day seems hard; well it's not if you know how to introduce few activities at a time instead of trying for everything simultaneously.

"The man who moves a mountain, begins by carrying away small stones"
Confucius

It is really simple if you look at it from this perspective. You might have heard or read that Confucius saying many times, but none of those times was when you are undergoing a self-transformational journey. I am sure you receive the message in it more consciously and understand it with more clarity.

We sometimes overthink everything and don't see our way towards our goals, this is because we are taught to focus on our goals and not how we reach them. At this moment, you need to figure out your next step, the set of new habits that you need to instill and they definitely will get you closer to your goal.

It is always possible to change your old habits or instill new habits, and for that to happen, you would need the 3 pillars of changing or instilling a habit:

Intention *, to mindfully set up, perform and observe the pillars of a habit (trigger – response – reward), until the habit becomes an automatic behavior.*

> **Discipline** *– in taking regular action without fail, especially when it gets tough. A desire to move towards your dream.*
>
> **21 days routine** *– to turn the action from mindful routine into an automatic behavior, hence a habit. Even if you feel that the new action has turned onto a habit prior to the end of the days, continue till the last just to besure.*

The human brain spends a huge chunk of the time imagining rewarding scenarios (most of which will not come to reality), and while doing that, your mind continuously scans your surroundings for potential rewards. The habit instilling process would depend so much on the reward that is attached to it, hence make sure you think of a reward that you will be strongly desiring to achieve, and making the reward easy to remember.

Take smokers for example, to name few of their triggers, they have the smoke with coffee, drinks, after food, during work breaks, etc. So as a response to these triggers, they light up a cigarette because they know the feeling they get from smoking, which the brain is interpreting as a reward.

By well defining the trigger and the reward, and by practicing the response for 21 days, it is guaranteed that the response will move from being a conscious action to becoming a subconscious reaction; in other words, an automatic behavior in response to a trigger, a new habit.

You can practice the same to improve some of the habits you already have, or to get rid of or change bad habits to good ones.
For that you would have to determine what you wanted to do but couldn't achieve no matter how much you tried. It is through your failures that you can identify the pattern and the habitual behavior, then visualize a solution, a scenario where you wouldn't fail, and you will see that you will stop responding the same way, and that will change both the way you proceed towards your goal and the outcome eventually.

Make sure the reward will have you stay motivated at all time, the lack of motivation will not lead to the same response/action every time a trigger is detected, and consequently you will be indirectly telling your brain that the response is not necessary because the reward is not sufficient.

Next page is a list of questions that by answering them in the most honest way possible, you would be able to understand yourself so much more and a new world would start unveiling itself without you doing anything, jus by writing down the true emotions and thoughts.

Ready your mind

Strengthen your rocks

Not too long ago, you were able to identify a list of thoughts and actions that we agreed to call your "rocks", on which you would go building your confidence and positive mindfulness.

As you already know, life – **like everything else** – has its ups and downs, its positive and negative. Since your rocks are vital for your progress and for your continuous mindfulness later on, it is now time to fortify these foundations.

In this chapter, you are going to concatenate all the knowledge received from previous chapters in order to boost your awareness.

It is no longer sufficient to listen to the recording you have done earlier in order to re-experience and reinforce your positive feelings. You ☺ ☐ are now on a more advanced level as you should know by now how to command your brain, meditate and create a routine in order to do turn these positive feelings into habits.

I want you to know that at this stage of your transformation, you have been liberated from your blocks, yet the feeling that you are still missing something is there. It is ok to feel this way; you have passed the caterpillar stage but still missing your wings to believe that you are a butterfly, hence the need of strengthening your rocks.

You can start by revisiting your "S" marked items, read them again and think of any other items you can add on the list. Most people keep on discovering themselves as they go forward. Now you can identify the feeling raised by each item and go ahead and write them next to each other.

The more positive feelings you could identify, the better. Some of the most common positive feelings and emotions are:

Love
Joy
Happiness
Pleasure
Curiosity
Amusement
Peacefulness
Amazement
Satisfaction

Don't forget the mantras and meditation sessions you have already started performing earlier, but on top of that you now need to up your game by addressing the most important but the most neglected side of you: Self-love.

Do not confuse self-love with ego. Ego is being very selfish, it is toxic and could cause you blind spots; Self-love comes from the heart, from projecting affection and warmth through yourself to others, it means having a high regard for your own. Self-love means being kind to yourself, not relinquishing your happiness for others, and always caring for yourself and your own interests.

In order to achieve self-love, you need to create your own activities, routines and meditation sessions that are focused on taking care of you, healing you, opening your heart and mind further, thus connecting you further to the universe, and the energy and resulting in supporting your physical, psychological, and spiritual evolution.

If you can't practice a sport that you love, then love a sport that you can practice (until you turn your life around and become able to have anything at your reach, including any sports facility you desire). At the moment, remember that any physical activity is better than sitting idle; don't allow yourself to neglect your body, and don't forget that the habit of sport is one of the greatest boosters of producing the hormones of happiness.

Walking and swimming are amongst the simplest and most affordable options as well the most successful in supporting active lifestyle. If you can't afford currently to go to fitness or sports facilities, there is no shortage of free of charge videos, demonstrating safe and steady practices of many sports you can do from home, targeted for different purposes (losing weight, burning fat, developing stamina, focusing on a special part of the body, meditation, breathing exercises etc.).

The only reason you are not using this opportunity (IF you are not using it), is you. Change your mindset now and take care of your body, your temple and your sanctuary. Do it for you.

The best way to cater to your psychological and spiritual side is meditation. Here's a recommended meditation dreamy session that shall help:

> *Get yourself into your meditative environment. The palms of your hands must be open, allowing you to send and receive energy.*
>
> *For this meditation session, your purpose is to focus on self-love.*
>
> *Do not set a timer, let everything happen organically, the longer this kind of sessions, the better the outcome.*
>
> *Before you close your eyes, make sure you concentrate on deep breathing.*
> *Close your eyes and after few very deep breaths, imagine you are able to fly to wherever you want in the universe.*
> *Fly to a safe place in your dream and make sure you are alone.*
>
> *Now visualize that you are able to have an out-of-body experience, where you can look at your body from the outside.*
>
> *Think of your body as a sacred temple that you are visiting. You should enter with utmost respect, affection and happiness.*
>
> *Note that the temple of your body has an altar in the center of your chest area.*
>
> *Go to that altar and place an object that represents pure love to you (for me it is the lotus flower).*
>
> *Now stand in front of that object and start streaming energy from a position of love, with light towards it; watch as it starts to change color and become lighter and brighter.*
>
> *Keep streaming energy and light till it becomes shiny, radiant and extremely bright that it's hard to look at it.*
>
> *At a certain point, there will be an explosion of light and this object will start emitting light from itself and will light up the whole temple.*
>
> *Feel the joy around you, the peace and serenity. Feel the blessing and the infinite energy that you just streamed from the universe into yourself.*
>
> *Once you feel ready to end the session, take few very deep breaths and come back to consciousness.*
> *Stay calm and seated (or better lay down for a while) and let the energy and the love sink in.*

Remember to always do everything with belief, focus, clear intentions and discipline, and keep reminding your brain that you are the boss.

The light you have gathered within you is your love for the universe, for yourself and for everything that is connected to you.

Make sure you remind yourself to do this every single day without exception, you keep going back to your temple and streaming endless love, light and energy. Continue doing it until you develop the habit of heightening your self-love to the new highest level each and every session; consequently, all your other rocks will become stronger in a much easier way once you get self-love going on with abundance.

Ready your mind

Actions speak louder

The famous expression *"actions speak louder than words"* simply means that people's actions reveal what they are made of, and they are far better than what they say. Generally speaking, this expression holds a call to do something positive. Actions and deeds are more reliable than words, even when the words are so articulate and affirmative. Actions hold results while words hold promises with the possibility that they might not be fulfilled.

The most common interpretation of this expression is that people prefer to see actions instead of hearing words. We however, are going to explore deeper explanations and meanings.

Consciousness is our vision, what our brain sees and receives, which is an illusion, while subconsciousness is what our true self, our heart and soul desire. As we often see in people, they say and promise one thing and then do something completely different. That is a prime example of brain, heart and soul not being connected and a person's desire to fit into somebody else's life plan by pleasing them. This is a sign that you are not aligned, you don't hear yourself, and you are not honest with yourself.

You might have noticed throughout your life that everyone you know – at a certain stage – said something, made a promise, released a statement about themselves or made plans and then, all of a sudden, all the words were gone with the wind, hence no action was performed.

I am sure you did too, I haven't encountered anyone who didn't. Try to remember a project idea that you decided to wait on until you have free time before starting to work on making it happen, then a while later the project was done by someone else or became obsolete. Or even a trip that you so much desired to take, but never saved up to pay for it and once you started saving years later, the deal ceased to exist or doubled in price making it very hard to buy.

All these examples and probably thousands more happen to a person in their lifetime, and by definition, postponing or delaying action till later is called procrastinating. We usually procrastinate actions and tasks we find hard, unpleasant, boring or stressful. If a task requires tremendous efforts or involves substantial amount of stress or anxiety, it's most probable we will avoid it.

Why is it that 99% of the time when you procrastinate, your goal becomes harder and sometimes almost impossible to achieve? It is because the universe does not favor procrastinators, yet it rewards those who act, it enables them to do more and sends more opportunities their way. You might have heard this in different words: *"Fortune favors the brave"* and i know you are just that.

Though it is not a personality attribute, it has been determined that it's one of the worst habits a person can have and if you detect it, you must immediately act on eliminating it. Procrastination will impair your process and everything else you would try to do in your life.

Pay highest attention to procrastination and always ensure to change minus to plus. Keep fighting it mindfully until you turn the situation around.

I am not saying that every idea or thought must be acted upon, you would then become overwhelmed with many tasks that might not be relevant; once you identify an action that will take you closer to a goal, take this action without hesitation, ensure to listen to your heart. Once you find a goal worth pursuing:

> *Align yourself and your mind with your goal.*
>
> *Start planning, thinking about and sending energy towards achieving your goal.*
>
> *Become one with your goal, like this you become more interested and invested in bringing it to reality.*
>
> *Educate yourself about your goal and develop the necessary knowledge that will help you get to the finish line with minimum mistakes and corrections.*
>
> *Visualize your goal (the brain doesn't recognize the difference between a real scene or a photo that you visualize). Once you visualize your goal you would start experiencing the emotions that would stem from the outcome.*
>
> *All the above steps would make you eager to get to the end result faster, and will entice you to take the required action in timely manner.*

Take daily actions, with every possibility and without hesitation. Taking happy and bold action and making decisions from your heart and with courage. If you succeed you move on to the second action and achieve more and more, and if you fail you adjust, nevertheless you learn something from your failure, yet keep this in mind: **"the biggest failure in life is not trying".** Even if you get a 100 times NO, 101 would be a YES and so big and amazing that would get all of your desires granted.

Ready your mind

Understanding yourself better

Knowing one's self is everyone's never-ending quest, but do we really get to absolutely know ourselves on a 100% basis? Studies of psychology, sociology and philosophy have addressed this point for centuries and none of the studies could produce a method that helps people to know themselves, or produce evidence of knowing themselves. There were always imperfections in the subject of study – people – that prevented them from perfectly knowing themselves: refusing to recognize one's ignorance about ones' self and flaws, lack of discipline or lack of self-control, are just a few to highlight.

Emphasizing these imperfections brings us to the conclusion that if we are not able to know who we are, then how can we determine who do we want to be, or even better, who we aim to be.

Well there is nothing to worry about, because instead of aiming to know yourself fully, try working towards understanding yourself better, it helps you make healthier decisions and build a more fulfilling life.

Remember that this guide is not helping you become perfect in the absolute meaning of the word, we have established earlier that such a state does not exist; This Guide is giving you tools for you to set your own goals, and navigate your own journey, and this one is an extremely important tool right here, since you will always be a work in progress, you will continuously need to redefine and improve some parts of yourself in order to understand yourself better.

Let us go through the main definitions of ***"know yourself better"***, as described by psychology and sociology. I recommend you write down your answers to the following:
"Discover your own unique personality"
                              "Determine your values and set your moral code"
"Decide what you want to be like in your future"
                              "Focus on your own interests and what you enjoy doing"
"Discover your strengths and weaknesses"

These are amazing and necessary steps to take. There are many online quizzes and heaps of specialists who could help you determine your personality type, and discovering your strengths and weaknesses, however, very few would address one very important point and even fewer would address it properly, and that point is your relationship with money. This is the part that is most important and forces you to get to know yourself at a deeper level than ever before.

Everybody wants to have money, lots of it, and if anyone pretends not to want money, they are lying to themselves and everyone else. I am not saying that money is the only thing to be pursued, but to deny your desire to have money is a big mistake.

Not many people understand why the flow of money towards them is blocked. In this context, there are 5 basics that if you get right, money will flow into your life with ease and abundance that you couldn't even imagine:

Make sure you understand and see the benefit of getting the benefit of any dream first for your own benefit and only then to others. Make sure your cup is full before you share with others.
Example:
You want a car
You see your car
You see yourself inside the car
You feel the engine roar and you love it
You love the exterior and the interior of this car
You love the colour of the car and how it makes you feel
You love that it is fast and light
"You MAYBE like the fact that you get attention in the car and some people are even jealous "

This last part marked with a star- this has to be after all of the above, as this point is not fully and really for YOU. It is ok and great to have the need to feel this BUT your emotions and feelings of appreciation and enjoyment HAVE to come first and above all.

The energy of money: *Money is a form of energy that is available for our use in order to afford the lifestyle we desire. It is always available around us as much as around other people, and there is enough of this energy for everyone to be rich, yet only a few notices it or choose to take. If we are operating on low energy, we will have little money that will always feel insufficient. If we are blocking any sort of energy to flow into our lives and bodies (no matter which sort, consciously or subconsciously), we are also blocking the flow of money energy. So, the first thing you need to work on is: Accept life as is and allow the inflow of energy.*

The fear of money: *Taking responsibility of your actions and thoughts, brings money into your life by opening the vision to more possibilities. Imagine a window of your car or house in need of a clean and that's exactly what we are doing with my method. It could be fear of not having enough money for everything we want to afford, fear of not receiving enough, fear of money flow disrupting and not restarting again, fear of having to protect this money once we have it, or any other fear that might be related to money. The universe senses your vibrations and interprets them as your desire, ending up with giving you according to your request. Universal rule is, whatever we give out, we receive, i.e. the more positive we give, the more positive we receive and the same goes for the negative.*

Money is hard work: *Here's another misconception that you need to rid yourself of. Abundance is not linked to hard work and to hard thinking and sleepless nights, it is rather a choice of how you allocate your energy and time in relation to money. In your mind, link money to prosperity and ease not to hardship.*

The use of money: *determine what you need the money for, ask for it, receive it, use it and ask for more and keep the flow going. It is very important to deal with money maturely, and always acknowledge that it is there for a purpose. If you ask to receive just for the sake of having money but not knowing what to do with it or not having determined the use for it, it is likely not to come. Set out a specific goal, act upon it and the money will follow.*

The money opportunities: *are everywhere you look, yet you are able to see money opportunity only if you are clear and honest with yourself. Allow the energy to flow in, don't give in to fear, acknowledge and believe that it is not hard to make money, and opportunity will present itself to you in a way that you can't ignore.*

Don't be shy to want money, talk about money and desire big money. Through passion, right energy and vibration you will invite it. Vibration is determined by our MOOD. The more positive are your thoughts the more radiant is your Mood, the bigger is your your light, the more gifts you would receive.

Understanding yourself better, especially being open and honest with yourself about money, is the most important step that you need to take in order to build the life or upgrade that you desire.

Ready your mind

You are the boss

By now, you can change the way you think and control the way you feel. You emphasize on the importance of daily exercises and activities towards your goals. Now it is the time for you to start becoming more effective with your time.

Have you ever wondered what is the most important formula that supports the success of all prosperous people and high performers?
Have you ever heard expressions like *"I am the master of my fate, the captain of my soul."*? Or *"I determine what my future will bring"*? or *"I can manifest whatever I desire"*? or *"your reality is based on what you believe"*? etc.

There are many exercises, tasks and texts in this book and in too many other books, motivational speeches, interviews with experts on the subject matter, videos and posts on social media, and TV programs that address manifestation, and the power of bringing your dreams and thoughts to reality, yet unfortunately very few would put sufficient emphasis on this short daily exercise that can and will change your life.

The simplicity of this exercise makes it barely believable that it has such an enormous impact on your day to day development, work, energy and life in general, you need to believe that it is very real.

It is the direct reflection of what you believe (at your core), and the proof that what you do every day matters. It is the practice of harnessing the power of your brain by letting it know – first thing when you open your eyes in the morning – that **you are the boss** of your mind. Fewer thoughts you have, more heart and intuition you feel, the more abundance comes.

Make sure you do not take this exercise lightly, and do it every single day without a break.

You can ask yourself before you go to sleep that you wish to do this exercise first thing in the morning, and your mind will find a way to remind you as you open your eyes. You can for sure use a reminder at the beginning, but it is best to rely on your intuition.

This exercise takes very few minutes of your time, and makes the rest of your day highly effective and magnificently productive. The indirect outcome of this exercise is employing the power of your own thoughts, to set the frequency of your brain and start sending signals to the universe and receiving information from the universal intelligence, all linked to your intentions, goals, dreams and desired future.

Here's a recommended meditation, dreamy session that you need to do in this context:
> *Get yourself into your meditative environment.*
>
> *The palms of your hands must be open, allowing you to send and receive energy.*
>
> *For this meditation session, your purpose is to tell your brain that* **You are the boss.**

Before you close your eyes, take a minute to think about everything you are grateful to have in life, picture what you are grateful for as you think about it and connect to the positive feelings attached to it.

Concentrate on deep breathing. The one that calms your mind and thoughts.

Close your eyes and visualize that you are able to have an out-of-body experience, where you can look at your body from the outside.

Visualize that you can hold your own brain with your own hands, do it with reverence, affection and joy.

Greet your brain with kind words and tell it the following:

I am very happy to meet and connect with you after all this time.
I am thankful for all that you have done for me so far.

I am proud of my achievements so far and I know that I need your continuous help to achieve more.

I am here to let you know that I am the boss from now on, and I have a plan, ready to act upon it and so it shall be.

I don't need the distractions and switching to different directions and subjects anymore.

I command you to stay focused.

I send you lots of love and energy and thank you again but I have to leave you now.

Put your brain where it was before and send some energy and loving light towards it till it becomes extremely bright.

Feel the blessing and the infinite energy that you just streamed from the universe into your brain.

Once you feel ready to end the session, take few very deep breaths and come back to consciousness.

Stay calm and seated and let the energy and the love sink in.

Make sure to remind your brain of what has worked for you and your accomplishments so far, and connect yourself to how great you felt and still feel about these achievements. This will subconsciously entice your mind to find ways and to take steps towards your goals that are set for that day, and ensure you achieve those goals.

The educational and social systems we have learned from so far, prompted us to always believe that the brain is the hard disk and operating system managing the intelligence in our bodies and lives; they taught us that whatever is recorded there and all the programs that we have are the result of years of experience, and always referred us to specialists in case we detected anomalies or the need of fixing anything.

What they forgot to tell us is that, we are also the programmers and network managers of this intelligent system, and we can control it and use it to our advantage and not the other way around.

Section 4

Mindful living

Mindful living

Awareness creates necessity for action

"We are born equal", and each has gone through their share of life tests and psychological conditioning, yet successful people differentiated themselves from the rest by the choices they made, their dedication and the mindset they adopted, each and every day of their lives.

Awareness helps us make better decisions. It boosts our self-confidence and adds clarity to our thoughts. It allows us to look at everything from different perspective, which leads us to become impartial and free from assumptions; by becoming brutally honest with ourselves so that it feels as if we are cleaning our windshield from all clouding thoughts, hence being able to build better lives and better relationships. All this enables to better see opportunities around us.

We are all connected to the source, but not everyone of us wants to exchange energy, signals and information because we all look for the simple way. Of course, it's easy to be lazy, but this doesn't lead you to your dream life. You and only you are responsible for your connection, are able to send and receive information and decide what to do with it. You need to choose to stay connected and repeat that choice regularly. Your brain is under your command and control. Disconnecting is going to confuse your mind by leading it to believe that you are not in control; this is where you allow your old patterns to start reappearing and damaging your projects and progress.

It is of highest importance to always acknowledge that life is not a walk in the park. You have chosen a life of greatness and gratitude, and that results in you choosing the road less traveled; your path will have obstacles and your willpower is going to be tested and only through awareness you will pass the tests, thus enabling yourself to continue maintaining and growing your wealth of both knowledge and possessions. You are more proactive rather than reactive with your life and decisions. Start using your energy for planning and executing more often instead of waiting for life to throw events at you and then you running to deal with the situation reactively.

Soon you will be aware of your reactions to life's situations, you will ask immediately the three questions mentioned previously in the Chapter called a "New set of daily mindful habits" and you would be able to react properly, being more composed and happier.

Sometimes, when life will test you, it will give you signs that you would be able to recognize easily by being aware. Most of the time, these signs will allow you a head start, a window of opportunity for preparing and planning, use this opportunity and never bury your head in the sand at the first sign of difficulty.

By ignoring the signs, acting complacently and thinking that nothing could affect you anymore, you are dropping your guards and allowing your mind to invite chaos back to your life. **Be careful, aware and vigilant about complacency, or be back to square one.**

Be ethical towards yourself and don't ignore your intuition and impulses.

As much as you are required to stay mindful, vigilant and proactive in order to prevent yourself from relapsing, I want you also to stay focused on awareness, you are absolutely getting used to being a winner, however be mindful to not allow your ego to get up to your head and make you think you are untouchable.
Earlier, you probably were lost, without a defined purpose, or you knew your purpose but were too lazy to pursue it, but now that you are aware and mindful, you have better choices. Now, you are able to savor your victories more often, and capitalize on them and the positive emotions associated to them.

Now you know that fear, stress and worrying don't help solve anything, so they are not an option for you. Now you have developed and advanced your emotional intelligence, your ability to understand, use, and manage your own emotions in productive ways; you are also able to empathize with others, help them deal with their emotions and overcome challenges and defuse conflict.

You are now capable of recognizing the life of excellence, and defining how to achieve it ethically. This comes with the rewards and the responsibility. You are responsible to act and demonstrate to yourself that you have the skills and habits required for excellence. You are also equipped with the tactics to improve your skills and habits of excellence.

So, in summary:

Your greatness comes from within, connect to it and stay connected.

Knowledge comes from the universe, connect to it and stay connected.

Tell your brain every day that you are the boss. Let it work for you and not the other way around.

Stay tuned for the signs given to you by the universe, and act upon them once they are received, don't ignore them.

Remind your brain and yourself about your achievements as often as possible.
Be proud of your achievements no matter how big or small they are.

Set goals for the day and work to achieve them every day.

Remind yourself of your purpose and long-term goals every day and don't let the road to achieving them become blurred.

Meditate, visualize, exercise and strive for excellence and don't settle for less.

Mindful living

Conclusion

What is the most accurate definition of becoming complete, of being whole? Yes, you read it correctly, the **most accurate definition**, because there is no absolute definition for that, at least not one understandable or acceptable to all of us.

Before we address the most accurate definition, let us take a quick scan to what has been said generally about wholeness and completeness, by ancient philosophers, enlightened ones and modern-day gurus and scientists.

The majority explained that for the human to become whole, he/she needs to be shattered and fragmented, then go through lots of repair, reconstruction and transformational work in the aim of becoming whole.

This is not a prerequisite and you don't need to wait till you hit rock bottom before you start rising. I know I haven't been broken nor have I hit – nor will I ever hit – rock bottom.

I had my fair share of ups and downs but I did not wait before taking matters into my own hands. You know you have the power, the knowledge to start proceeding and now the awareness, so spread your wings and fly.

Here is some ideologies and quotes from the past that you might enjoy:

> Wholeness depends only on ones' self, without the need of another person.

> Learning acceptance. *"Once you learn accepting vulnerabilities in yourself and others, all the cracks and imperfections, you become whole".*

> Connecting to the inner self and others. *"You can only be connected to others if you are connected to yourself and the truth inside".*

> Connect to and trust the universe. *"The way to become one with the universe is to trust it".*

> Respect and kindness to others. *"Set an example. Treat everyone with respect even those who don't deserve it; not as a reflection of their character, but as a reflection of yours".*

> Loving and valuing yourself. *"you are not a drop in the ocean, you are the entire ocean in a drop".*

> Loving and valuing others. *"To possess a rich life of wholeness is to show loving and caring characteristics toward others".*

All the above is true, but incomplete. It is incomplete because it addresses many characteristics but separately, while wholeness shall encompass everything.

It is true that you need only yourself to become complete, and that is in terms of the material you need to build your wholeness. It is not absolutely true though that you need no one else; I am not sure about the statement that we were made perfect, either it lacks the truth in defining perfection, or it lacks perfection in defining the truth.

So, in order to become whole, we need to connect to ourselves, our powers and uniqueness, and we need to continuously work on refining and widening our knowledge about ourselves.

We need to connect to the universe through meditations, thoughts, intentions and actions and we need to always do that with the respect, pride and confidence we owe to ourselves, as well as the humility we owe to the greatness of the universe with which we are becoming one.

We need to connect to others through all forms of exchange known to be practical, honorable and respectable to mankind. We are social beings and the interaction with others is an extension of ourselves to others and through others, and it is crucial for our lives, our energies and our infinity.

We need to connect to all forms of life not only mankind. Be it plants or animals, we need to treat all other forms of life with reverence because we are part of them and they of us. We eat them, breath them and share all the natural resources with them and if we don't treat that with respect, then we cannot become whole.

We need to connect to the energy of things that form our ecosystems, habitat, means of transportation, and all other means available for us to conduct life and living, with an emphasis on money that is practically the basic component of any form of exchange and trade since the failing of the barter system.

My method is unique, not only because it described wholeness from all these perspectives united, but also because it has one narrative that is the same, all the way throughout the journey and that is: *"If you do everything from the position of love and respect to yourself, hence to others, you realize that you are **number one**, you then also realize that you are whole".*

When you realize that you candidly love yourself, and **when you accept that physically and spiritually you are part of something bigger,** and you accept that you come from something/somewhere, you would stop living the classical life of fighting with everyone about everything and you would implement the position of love with all you do, because you know and understand that by doing everything everyday with love, you are loving yourself ultimately, you don't need anything anymore and you are complete. Staying posetive and happy equals abundance and fortune.

Mindful living

Subconscious growth of self

Your next realization after having learned how to become whole, is to liberate your soul and attain your subconscious growth. That is to become unconstrained by social ties and structures as traditionally known, to become self-centered and independent.

Here is another time to remind you that you are number one. At some stages of your journey, you must have learned – but might have as well forgotten – that you are not living your life according to what others plan and design for you or as they desire to see you living. The time comes again to remind you of that with an emphasis and a slightly different and more mature point of view.

You are no longer seeking your independence to prove anything to yourself or anyone; you rather know by now that you are independent, you embrace your spontaneity, and refuse to live your life according to the conventional ways that kept you inside the box for so many years.

With the awareness of this freedom, you begin to look at all types of social bonds from a different point of view and understand them with more depth. It becomes very easy for you to enjoy the rewards and fruits of healthy relationships, that are built on the foundation of understanding and respecting each other, and not the simple illusions that come with the classical proposition of "love". I am not saying that love is bad, on the contrary it is necessary, but when love stands alone, it fades away, or worst it turns into a source of disturbance due to connections built basically on emotions and not rationale.

The old belief of depending on others or needing others has to disappear if you still didn't dispose of it. It is unnecessary to stay in any kind of relatiship because of blood or family ties, or the time spent and great memories, or what you have been through together or for the sake of anything else for that matter; any rapport that has been or has become toxic to you must be repaired or cease to exist; either way, it must stop sucking your energy. Only happy and pleasant has to survive.

Don't take this as a suggestion that you should end all relationships, instead make sure you address things that aren't to your satisfaction. From a position of LOVE speak about how you would like things to be different to the other participant, what changes you would like to be implemented by both parties in order to repair and/or reconstruct your bonds on new basis and with new rules. Setting boundaries is pleasant and productive and always received well, IF you speak from a position of LOVE and calm mind. Dont forget we are all vibrational beings.

It is important that the other party gets to recognize the following:

You respect and appreciate the time they have been in your life, but respect more the time left in yours.

You now have restructured your life and mind and prepped yourself for success. No more space for unnecessary drama.

You have no fear to continue your life on your own.

You are more than enough and don't depend on anything or anyone.

Your success poses no threat to your relation with them, unless they start feeling threatened by it and start sabotaging it (regardless if knowingly or not).

Your continuing to be in their life is based on your conscious decision, your commitment to yourself and to them, as well as the respect that you owe to yourself and to them.
Their continuing to be in your life is based on reciprocity and that you will settle for nothing less.

Anyone who has high self-esteem and who respects you, should be thrilled to know they are appreciated by you and that you wish them to stay in your life, and anyone who lets their ego, distorted understanding of life and their defensiveness stand between the both of you are not worthy of your time and energy.

This concept should simply be applied to all types of social relationships: Direct family members, relatives, childhood friends, best friends, close and dear neighbors, spouse, partner, better half, etc. It is your call at the end because you are the boss; I would recommend that you at least run a thorough analysis of the people that you consider your close circle and see if anyone isn't fit to be there.

Out of experience, and with proven results of social experiments, the biggest challenge for an individual is having to change their behavior and sometimes their plans in order to fit in, to meet expectations of their social environment, and the people in their lives. Osho Gita once said: "your whole idea about yourself is borrowed - borrowed from those who have no idea of who they are themselves."

When you apply wholeness, awareness and subconscious growth, you stop being a hurdle in your own path, and you start using the power to deal with anyone or anything that might stand in your way. What you do with this power and how you use it is entirely your decision as it is only directed by calm mind and happiness within.

Mindful living

Trust the universe

I will not go on too much in this chapter, because even if I did, I can't teach you how to trust; it has to come from within, from a decision to just do it, from passion for life, passion for youself, for your tasks and progress; once you have that passion, trust comes into your life and you learn to trust yourself, people and the universe.

What I would like to do is to express only the importance of understanding the rationale behind trusting the universe.

When you start trusting the universe, you start enforcing your belief that you are number one, that you are in unity with the universe and that you are whole and ready, you wont need anyones opinion or approval in order to act.

You start explicitly expressing your acceptance of the universe's unpredictable ways, and acknowledging that it has powers that interfere and play a very important role in everyone's life. You would eventually admit that you are helpless in many situations and that would lead to you changing the way you live and stop worrying. You would start seeing life events into two major categories:

The ones you can't control and you can't do nothing about, so worrying would not help.

The ones you can do something about, and instead of worrying you would act upon.

This will save you a great deal of time and energy that you use to spend by worrying. People would call that "not sweating the small stuff" but I call that being smart and aware.

When you trust the universe, you would start seeing clear and noticing what belongs to you and what doesn't, to what you should react and what doesnt need nor deserve your attention. By listening to your intuition, you would stop devoting your time and energy on pursuits that would not lead to your desired destination and goals, no time wasting. You would cut your losses and invest no further in businesses and people that are not bringing you happiness.

You would start becoming more grateful and appreciative of what you have, hence you would highlight to the universe your belief that something bigger is coming, and that you are both happy and blessed to be able to pursue your destiny and your higher self. The universe would keep rewarding you further but you need to be patient and keep your faith.

You need to be patient, because despite all what you do, you don't have complete view of the bigger picture, hence things shall happen as per the timing meant for them. Do your part and the universe will answer.

While being patient, the universe will keep testing you and listening to your vibrations, so, keep moving and proactively taking all necessary action.

You would surrender to the fact that in the universe there is randomness and sometimes chaos, and by accepting this very fact, you open your mind and heart to everything, and allow the energies of life to flow into yours gracefully and without interruption.

In fact, this is how the law of attraction works. When you do what you are supposed to do and you trust the universe wholeheartedly, the universe will bring the right people and the right opportunities into your life when the time is right, even sometimes it might seem late but it will eventually come when you are ready.

Trust the universe as it is you, it will always have your back and take care of you. It is the most powerful ally one can have.

Section 5

Recap

Recap

Finding your happy place

As established previously, this book is equipping you with necessary tools for you to use your plans and goals by acting without fear and a need of approval. By doing this you are guaranteed to multiply your income.

For your knowledge to be effectively implemented, you would need to keep in the forefront of your thoughts, plans and actions the following three points:

> **Discipline:** *It's the foundation on which you build everything that you cherish and value, and it is your ability to control your emotions and defeat your limitations. Your determination is the only thing that keeps you consistent and* **without discipline, you relinquish being in control of what you are doing in life and how you are doing it***, you start procrastinating again and when life events start taking over, you find yourself going back to places you don't desire to be at.*

> **Results and rewards:** *A very important point that people tend to ignore as they plan for the future. It is a given that one must have long-term goals that should be specific, meaningful, and realistic. Also, a clear vision, planning, discipline and continued efforts are needed to help stick with your long-term goals, and anticipate ways to handle adverse scenarios. It is of colossal significance to know that short-term goals are as important as the long-term goals. Behavioral psychology shows that people react positively to achievements and rewards, they stay motivated by them. If you regularly set short-term goals that are achievable (I am by no means saying very easy and lazy short-term goals), you'll be highly likely to stay motivated, disciplined and continue to put efforts towards your long-term goals. Short-term goals also minimize procrastination and enable you to focus on one thing at a time. This focus will show you that your actions have a sense of purpose, and you'll be less likely to get discouraged. Short-term goals provide the foundation for something greater so don't hesitate to breakdown your long-term goals into short-term steps, milestones and tasks and by all means.* **Make sure you reward yourself for all your achievements and results. YOU DESERVE IT & YOU NEED IT.**

> **Compete against yourself:** *You need to always seek something to ascend for, a place that is beyond frustration and all negativity, somewhere where you feel happy. You think you would achieve that through discipline, results and rewards but this is far from being the complete truth. No matter how long the period you have set for your long-term goals, you must hope that you would not only achieve them but also outlive them; so, a very important question you should always ask yourself after having reached any goals:* **"where would I like to go from here?".** *The answer is not always clear, most people would start comparing themselves to others and by doing that they distort the reality. I tell you the most important for us to stay on a healthy course is to always thrive to improve our lives, by trying to always to become the best versions of ourselves. No matter what you have achieved, never allow yourself to stop evolving and reach stagnation instead.*

When you reach the stage of your life where the above three points constitute your modus operandi, you become unstoppable. There is nothing you would not be able to achieve if you put the planning, work and efforts, the discipline, the achievements and rewards and you stay adaptable, ready to adjust your routes or yourself for the sake of your own betterment.
Again, I remind you to focus always on a very important fact: you are number one and you are more than enough. Keep focusing on yourself, your life and your goals until you find your happy place.

Money can't buy happiness they say; If you keep in mind that money is only a tool that makes our life more comfortable and that is where the importance of money comes from, you would realize that money can't buy happiness but is does make life much more fun to live. Always remember, that your happiness is not measured by your net-worth, but by the happy times and memories. My final advice to you, **whenever you feel happy, seek to be happier and make that your goal and final destination. There is always room for improvement especially when you have the money to make it that much more entertaining. Make sure you never lose passion as it is the key to success and fortune. Your mindset determines the outcome of each day!**

Authors' closing note

My desire is for this book to be so popular that billions of people are able to read it, several times and change their perspective of the life they have. Once they do that, the world would open up like an oyster shell and all you then need to do is to decide and step out into this amazing world that we call home. My Dream is to be able to show every reader, how amazingly beautiful this planet is, through my eyes.

*<u>**I LOVE** ME, **I LOVE** YOU,
I LOVE LIFE.</u>*

*<u>FOREVER AND EVER GRATEFUL TO ALL,
THEN, NOW AND IN THE FUTURE.</u>*

Here I come xo…

Olga Cooper
30.06.2022

<u>INSTAGRAM</u>

Thanks to the following stars this book has come out to light:

My husband and partner Giovanni PALMA
Editor David BUCHANAN Allifax CANADA
Graphic Design STUDIO TANGRAM Como ITALY

www.ingramcontent.com/pod-product-compliance
Lightning Source LLC
Chambersburg PA
CBHW040235220526
45473CB00001B/247